The Book of **Dog Poems**

First published in Great Britain in 2021
by Laurence King Publishing
an imprint of The Orion Publishing Group Ltd
Carmelite House, 50 Victoria Embankment
London EC4Y 0DZ

An Hachette UK Company

1 3 5 7 9 10 8 6 4 2

A CIP catalogue record for this book is
available from the British Library.

ISBN 978 1 78627 943 9

Commissioning editor: Elen Jones
Senior editor: Gaynor Sermon
Design: Florian Michelet
Poetry clearance: Whitefox

Repro house: Fine Arts Repro, Hong Kong
Printer: C&C Offset Printing Company Ltd

Printed in China

Laurence King Publishing is committed to ethical
and sustainable production. We are proud
participants in The Book Chain Project®
bookchainproject.com

www.laurenceking.com
www.orionbooks.co.uk

# The Book of **Dog Poems**

*Sarah Maycock & Ana Sampson*

Laurence King Publishing

# Contents

# Introduction

'The better I get to know men,
   the more I find myself loving dogs'
*Charles de Gaulle*

If you have ever shared your life with a dog, you'll
understand why the famous French former premier
purportedly made this remark. It's hard to imagine
even the most committed lover or the most adoring
family member shouting with dizzy joy and excitement
every single time you return home from an errand.
Yet your dog will never let your arrival pass without
wild celebration and will never roll its eyes when you
suggest spending time together. To live with a dog is to
have not just a friend, but a dedicated and enthusiastic
cheerleader in your corner.

The poems collected in this book celebrate dogs of
all ages – from the frisking puppy to the grizzled and
venerable hound. They imagine a dog's-eye view of the
world: the tasty puddles, the stories written in scent,
the pity felt – as Chesterton's dog Quoodle says – for the
noselessness of poor man, who can't smell the birds'
breath. The almost infinite variety of dogs, too, is found
within these pages, from the chic and cherished 'petits
chiens de Paris' immortalised by Helen Burke, to the
rangy wolfish loner roaming the town's wild outskirts,
maddened by the moon. Their expressions are both

keenly observed and lovingly relayed, including the curious attention of Lawrence Ferlinghetti's 'Dog', head cocked quizzically like 'a living questionmark'.

Elizabeth Barrett Browning and D. H. Lawrence are among the writers who are – often somewhat rudely – awoken by their pets. Lawrence's incorrigible Bibbles tears in 'like a little black whirlwind'. Hardwicke Drummond Rawnsley's poem 'We Meet at Morn, My Dog and I' beautifully describes an early morning scene that many dog owners will recognise: the tail drumming on the bedroom door, the half-shout, and the desperate scuffle before his pet flings itself into the room. Owner and dog greet each other – one yawning and the other in an ecstasy of excitement, swearing 'fresh love and fealty' for the day ahead.

Writers have here captured the mad rapture of a dog galloping, racing 'across morning-wet grass, high-fiving the day' as in Lisa Oliver's 'Flight'. W. H. Auden once said, 'In times of joy, all of us wished we possessed a tail we could wag'. One of the reasons our dogs inspire such happiness is their deep and physical expressions of delight. Their naked enthusiasm is balm in a cynical and sardonic age, in which we sometimes feel we have shed simple joy with childhood. The ecstasy they radiate is infectious. Harold Monro's wonderful 'Dog' is a litany of easy pleasures: the thrill of a walk, then heading home to the further joy of food to be bolted, drowsing to the chat of your people and sinking, untroubled, into the 'bed-delicious hours of night'. Dogs remind us – as in Mark Doty's 'Golden Retrievals' – to live with both feet in the present, to taste and savour the day without fretting about yesterday or tomorrow, to cherish the here and now.

The pleasure of exercising the dog is examined within these pages, too. There are roads to ramble and woods to wander, puddles and ponds to lap and a world of exciting smells to track in the countryside, and fire hydrants and flea markets to tempt the sophisticated urban canine.

Not all of these dogs are well trained. There is plenty of mischief in these mutts. Dorothy Parker, Rupert Brooke and Jo Shapcott celebrate the naughty dogs, the dirty dogs, the snappers and the scrappers, the destroyers of shoes and newly made beds and nippers of calves. But here, too, are working dogs such as the trusty huskies, strong and solid and ready to run.

Dogs remind us that to be with those we love is the most holy of pleasures. The agony of being apart is expressed, beautifully, in several of these poems, as is the utterly joyous nature of the subsequent reunion, for both parties. The loyalty of the pet who waits for long, lonely years like Pope's Argus is matched by that of the suburban pup to whom the working day seems a desolate century, and both are transfigured with wagging happiness to be reunited with their people.

We close this collection with farewells. Poets have, for hundreds and hundreds of years, been moved to remember their canine companions with some of the most heart-rending verse ever written. The death of such a staunch friend and constant companion is no small sorrow, the poets tell us. It is right to mourn them as they deserve.

I hope there will be a cocked head, an excited squeak, a trailing tongue or a bright eye here that you will recognise. Our dogs can't know how many passionate pages they have unwittingly inspired, but as long as there are walks and woods and puddles and cuddles and, afterwards, warm feet to sprawl on while you read about them, it will have been a good dog day.

Ana Sampson

# Rehomer's Prayer

*Di Slaney*

Bring me the wobbly, the scabby, the beaten,
the oldies, the lost, the could-have-been-eaten,
the wayward, the strays, the nightmares to tame,
the cringers, the timid, the ones with no name,
the mangy, the lousy, the missing-one-leg,
the dirty, the stinky, the too-tired-to-beg,
the crooked, the toothless, the eartorn, the humped,
the knobbly, the limping, the recently-dumped,
the feral, the fearful, the head- and hand-shy,
the last gasp no-hopers, the ones who might die,
the three-homes-already, the stubborn returners,
the deafened, the sightless, the never-will-learners,
the tucked-in-the-corner, the sodden in pee,
bring me all these ones – please, bring them to me.

# Dog, on First Being Named

*Jane Commane*

They're wrong, of course, our owners who think
they own us; choice an illusion, out of their hands
quicker than a quicksilver whippet out the traps.

But the name at least, this two-syllable moniker,
and the telephone manner with which you deliver it,
is yours to give, a password for recall, bringing me to heel

and to your hand's peace offering, rubber-nosing your scent
to sniff out invisible trails of all your laughter and grievings,
of daffodils and thunder, the rec's muddy turf, thawing snow.

From this first, it's your voice that cracks instinct, unlocks obedience, echoes through each leg-twitching dream, pursued across each field; you naming our bond, my wordless joy.

Later, you teach me code words for how I must ask, lie, play dead. But it's my name I'll chase down, hounding to your cry, in the long over-arm pitch of all the dog days to come.

# *from* Macbeth

*William Shakespeare (1564–1616)*

Ay, in the catalogue ye go for men,
As hounds and greyhounds, mongrels, spaniels, curs,
Shoughs, water-rugs, and demi-wolves are clept
All by the name of dogs. The valued file
Distinguishes the swift, the slow, the subtle,
The housekeeper, the hunter, every one
According to the gift which bounteous nature
Hath in him closed, whereby he does receive
Particular addition, from the bill
That writes them all alike. And so of men.
Now, if you have a station in the file,
Not i' th' worst rank of manhood, say 't,
And I will put that business in your bosoms,
Whose execution takes your enemy off,
Grapples you to the heart and love of us,
Who wear our health but sickly in his life,
Which in his death were perfect.

# A Little Dog Sense

*Sue Hardy-Dawson (b. 1963)*

If I had a dog's ears I could hear leaves falling in a wood
catch the sound of a snail's tears
appreciate a sparrow's sneeze
the tiniest splash of the first raindrop
and listening without looking always tell who was
    at the door

If I had a dog's nose I could smell badger's trail on
    the ground
the faint trace of fox and hare
relish the aroma of breeze
delight in dirt and a river's dank stink
and with the power of sniffing know where a cat
    crossed before

If I had a dog's tongue I could taste puddles and think
    them good
recall fondly – tang of worm
the faint flavour of handkerchiefs
savour the sweetness of salad of sock
and with my delicate palate appreciate grey crumbs
    from the floor

If I had a dog's eyes I could see the twitch of a rat's foot
at dusk – a shadowy form
seven ways your face moves in sleep

the strange shapes of anger and of laughter
and with my shortness of sight all the clues that you
    unknowingly wear

If I had a dog's touch I could feel each morning getting up
the gentle heartbeat of calm
difference in different feet
a distant railway rumbling the earth
and with the softest of paws the thudding of gates and
    return of cars

But if I'd a dog's voice I must bark tell all with a tail's wag
I might miss my talking hands
and what is it that a dog dreams
to go only where others can in the world
with no will but what they're told. No these are things
    I could never wish for

# The Song of the Dog Quoodle

*G. K. Chesterton (1874–1936)*

They haven't got no noses,
The fallen sons of Eve,
Even the smell of roses
Is not what they supposes,
But more than mind discloses,
And more than men believe.

They haven't got no noses,
They cannot even tell
When door and darkness closes
The park old Gluck encloses
Where even the Law of Moses
Will let you steal a smell.

The brilliant smell of water,
The brave smell of a stone,
The smell of dew and thunder,
The old bones buried under,
Are things in which they blunder
And err, if left alone.

The wind from winter forests,
The scent of scentless flowers,
The breath of brides' adorning,
The smell of snare and warning,
The smell of Sunday morning
God gave to use for ours.

And Quoodle here discloses
All things that Quoodle can,
They haven't got no noses,
They haven't got no noses,
And goodness only knowses
The Noselessness of Man.

# Flush or Faunus

*Elizabeth Barrett Browning (1806–1861)*

You see this dog?  It was but yesterday
I mused forgetful of his presence here,
Till thought on thought drew downward tear on tear,
When from the pillow, where wet-cheeked I lay,
A head, as hairy as Faunus, thrust its way
Right sudden against my face, – two golden-clear
Great eyes astonished mine, – a drooping ear
Did flap me on either cheek to dry the spray!
I started first, as some Arcadian,
Amazed by goatly god in twilight grove;
But, as the bearded vision closelier ran
My tears off, I knew Flush, and rose above
Surprise and sadness, – thanking the true Pan,
Who, by low creatures, leads to heights of love.

# *from* Bibbles

*D. H. Lawrence (1885–1930)*


Not that you're merely a softy, oh dear me no.
You know which side your bread is buttered.
You don't care a rap for anybody.
But you love lying warm between warm human thighs,
    indiscriminate,
And you love to make somebody love you, indiscriminate,
You love to lap up affection, to wallow in it,
And then turn tail to the next comer, for a new dollop.

And start prancing and licking and cuddling again,
    indiscriminate.

Oh yes, I know your little game.

Yet you're so nice,
So quick, like a little black dragon.
So fierce, when the coyotes howl, barking like a whole little
    lion, and rumbling,
And starting forward in the dusk, with your little black fur
    all bristling like plush
Against those coyotes, who would swallow you like
    an oyster.

And in the morning, when the bedroom door is opened,
Rushing in like a little black whirlwind, leaping straight as
    an arrow on the bed at the pillow

And turning the day suddenly into a black tornado
    of *joie de vivre*, Chinese dragon.

So funny
Lobbing wildly through deep snow like a rabbit,
Hurtling like a black ball through the snow,
Champing it, tossing a mouthful,
Little black spot in the landscape!

So absurd
Pelting behind on the dusty trail when the horse sets
    off home at a gallop:
Left in the dust behind like a dust-ball tearing along
Coming up on fierce little legs, tearing fast to catch up,
    a real little dust-pig, ears almost blown away,
And black eyes bulging bright in a dust-mask
Chinese-dragon-wrinkled, with a pink mouth grinning,
    under jaw shoved out
And white teeth showing in your dragon-grin as you
    race, you split-face,
Like a trundling projectile swiftly whirling up,
Cocking your eyes at me as you come alongside,
    to see if I'm on the horse,
And panting with that split grin,
All your game little body dust-smooth like a little pig,
    poor Pips.

# We Meet At Morn, My Dog and I

*Hardwicke Drummond Rawnsley (1851–1920)*

Still half in dream, upon the stair I hear
A patter coming nearer and more near,
And then upon my chamber door
A gentle tapping,
For dogs though proud are poor,
And if a tail will do to give command
Why use a hand?
And after that, a cry, half sneeze, half yapping,
And next a scuffle on the passage floor,
And then I know the creature lies to watch
Until the noiseless maid will lift the latch,
And like a spring
That gains its power by being tightly stayed,
The impatient thing
Into the room
Its whole glad heart doth fling,
And ere the gloom
Melts into light and window blinds are rolled,
I hear a bounce upon the bed,
I feel a creeping towards me – a soft head,
And on my face
A tender nose and cold –
That is the way, you know, that dogs embrace –

And on my hand like sun-warmed rose-leaves flung,
The least faint flicker of the warmest tongue,
 – And so my dog and I have met and sworn
Fresh love and fealty for another morn.

# Flight

*Lisa Oliver*


We breathe into sleep, the low rumble of rain
    on the roof,
the soft pulse of blood lullabying us.
Floor boards in our emptied house creak half-heard,
    and I sink
into the hinterland, neither here nor there.

I wake to the thud of the newspaper, the gurgle
    of the heating.
I lie for a while. Half-remembered dreams scutter
back into the dark but the taste of them lingers
like salt on my tongue.

You are still sleeping so I creep down the stairs,
silence the kettle before it alarms you.
I hold the mug in my hands,
let it warm them.

I watch two summer-fat blackbirds breakfast
    on berries,
stripping the tree, whilst in the leaves,
a shoal of sparrows
dart and flash.

The dog races across morning-wet grass, high-fiving
    the day
He barks and dances a circle. The birds scatter
at the sound of him. I shield my eyes
as I watch them fly.

# I Started Early

*Emily Dickinson (1830–1886)*


I started Early – Took my Dog –
And visited the Sea –
The Mermaids in the Basement
Came out to look at me –

And Frigates – in the Upper Floor
Extended Hempen Hands –
Presuming Me to be a Mouse –
Aground – upon the Sands –

But no Man moved Me – till the Tide
Went past my simple Shoe –
And past my Apron – and my Belt
And past my Boddice – too –

And made as He would eat me up –
As wholly as a Dew
Upon a Dandelion's Sleeve –
And then – I started – too –

And He – He Followed – close behind –
I felt His Silver Heel
Upon my Ancle – Then My Shoes
Would overflow with Pearl –

Until We met the Solid Town –
No One He seemed to know –
And bowing – with a Mighty look –
At me – The Sea withdrew –

# Roads

*Amy Lowell (1874–1925)*

I know a country laced with roads,
They join the hills and they span the brooks,
They weave like a shuttle between broad fields,
And slide discreetly through hidden nooks.
They are canopied like a Persian dome
And carpeted with orient dyes.
They are myriad-voiced, and musical,
And scented with happiest memories.
O Winding roads that I know so well,
Every twist and turn, every hollow and hill!
They are set in my heart to a pulsing tune
Gay as a honey-bee humming in June.
'T is the rhythmic beat of a horse's feet
And the pattering paws of a sheep-dog bitch;
'T is the creaking trees, and the singing breeze,
And the rustle of leaves in the road-side ditch.

A cow in a meadow shakes her bell
And the notes cut sharp through the autumn air,
Each chattering brook bears a fleet of leaves
Their cargo the rainbow, and just now where
The sun splashed bright on the road ahead
A startled rabbit quivered and fled.
O Uphill roads and roads that dip down!

You curl your sun-spattered length along,
And your march is beaten into a song
By the softly ringing hoofs of a horse
And the panting breath of the dogs I love.
The pageant of Autumn follows its course
And the blue sky of Autumn laughs above.

And the song and the country become as one,
I see it as music, I hear it as light;
Prismatic and shimmering, trembling to tone,
The land of desire, my soul's delight.
And always it beats in my listening ears
With the gentle thud of a horse's stride,
With the swift-falling steps of many dogs,
Following, following at my side.
O Roads that journey to fairyland!
Radiant highways whose vistas gleam,
Leading me on, under crimson leaves,
To the opaline gates of the Castles of Dream.

# *from* The Invitation: To Tom Hughes

*Charles Kingsley (1819–1875)*

Do the work that's nearest,
Though it's dull at whiles,
Helping, when we meet them,
Lame dogs over stiles;
See in every hedgerow
Marks of angels' feet,
Epics in each pebble
Underneath our feet;
Once a year, like schoolboys,
Robin-Hooding go,
Leaving fops and fogies
A thousand feet below.

# Dog

*Harold Monro (1879–1932)*


You little friend, your nose is ready; you sniff,
Asking for that expected walk,
(Your nostrils full of the happy rabbit-whiff)
And almost talk.

And so the moment becomes a moving force;
Coats glide down from their pegs in the humble dark;
The sticks grow live to the stride of their vagrant course.
You scamper the stairs,
Your body informed with the scent and the track and the mark
Of stoats and weasels, moles and badgers and hares.

We are going OUT. You know the pitch of the word,
Probing the tone of thought as it comes through fog
And reaches by devious means (half-smelt, half-heard)
The four-legged brain of a walk-ecstatic dog.

Out in the garden your head is already low.
(Can you smell the rose? Ah, no.)
But your limbs can draw
Life from the earth through the touch of your padded paw.

Now, sending a little look to us behind,
Who follow slowly the track of your lovely play,
You carry our bodies forward away from mind
Into the light and fun of your useless day.

Thus, for your walk, we took ourselves, and went
Out by the hedge and the tree to the open ground.
You ran, in delightful strata of wafted scent,
Over the hill without seeing the view;
Beauty is smell upon primitive smell to you:
To you, as to us, it is distant and rarely found.

Home ... and further joy will be surely there:
Supper waiting full of the taste of bone.
You throw up your nose again, and sniff, and stare
For the rapture known

Of the quick wild gorge of food and the still lie-down
While your people talk above you in the light
Of candles, and your dreams will merge and drown
Into the bed-delicious hours of night.

# The Little White Dog

*May Ellis Nichols (1862–1948)*

Little white dog with the meek brown eyes,
Tell me the boon that most you prize.
Would a juicy bone meet your heart's desire?
Or a cozy rug by a blazing fire?
Or a sudden race with a truant cat?
Or a gentle word? Or a friendly pat?
Is the worn-out ball you have always near
The dearest of all the things held dear?
Or is the home you left behind
The dream of bliss to your doggish mind?
But the little white dog just shook his head
As if 'None of these are best,' he said.

A boy's clear whistle came from the street;
There's a wag of the tail and a twinkle of feet,
And the little white dog did not even say,
'Excuse me, ma'am,' as he scampered away;
But I'm sure as can be his greatest joy
Is just to trot behind that boy.

# Golden Retrievals

*Mark Doty (b. 1950)*

Fetch? Balls and sticks capture my attention
seconds at a time. Catch? I don't think so.
Bunny, tumbling leaf, a squirrel who's – oh
joy – actually scared. Sniff the wind, then

I'm off again: muck, pond, ditch, residue
of any thrillingly dead thing. And you?
Either you're sunk in the past, half our walk,
thinking of what you never can bring back,

or else you're off in some fog concerning
 – tomorrow, is that what you call it? My work:
to unsnare time's warp (and woof!), retrieving,
my haze-headed friend, you. This shining bark

a Zen master's bronzy gong, calls you here,
entirely, now: bow-wow, bow-wow, bow-wow.

# They (May Forget (Their Names (If Let Out)))

*Vahni Capildeo (b. 1973)*

petcitement incitement of a pet to excitement
petcitement incitement into the excitement
of being a pet petcitement incitement to be
a pet a fed pet a fleece pet incitement to be
a floorpet a fleapit a carpet a polkadot
blanket pet blanket pet answer brass doorbell what name
tin waterbowl what name thrilled vomitfall polkadot
padded on patted on turded on welcome mat name
turns to no one's reminder walks wilder walks further
downriver from calling calling owner predator
who that who tagalong meaner whose canines further
from food fleece floor flea cloth car poll card dot blank bit door
no no owner owns in nomine domini pet
outruns petfetch petcome will wild default reset

# Uncertainty is Not a Good Dog

*Jo Shapcott (b. 1953)*


Uncertainty is not a good dog.
She eats bracken and sheep shit,
drops her litters in foxholes
and rolls in all the variables,

wriggling on her back, until
she reeks of them,
until their scents are her scents.
She takes sudden, windy routes

through hummocks, cairns and ditches
so you can't spot where she is
and acknowledge her velocity
at the same time. She's fidgety,

but still careful to snuffle
through all the mud on the trail.
She can't see in the dark
but bumps her snout

on the overhang lapping
the path. Daylight's no better:
she has to screw her eyes
tight against the glare

and, panting, just risk it, following
her nose across the landscape
her tongue brighter than probability,
brighter than heather, winberry and scree.

# Black Dog

*Alison Brackenbury (b. 1953)*


Cold broods over the house, like a white stare.
Across the lamps' lights, snow sprays feathers – stars –
You grind your blue shoes in my lap
All your new books are read.
     But there are stories
Which drift, before we sleep, as far away
As lonely barns, from which the crumbled straw
Spills snow on frozen ground. Here is a story
Without a start or end, from the flat land
From which I came.
     Now listen – You love dogs
The lumbering St Bernard, prancing Cairn –
A man is walking up a clouded lane
Head hot with drink; the night. What makes him turn?
High as the hedge, it stands. It watches him.
Its eyes are vast as stars.
     On the low road
Skimming the dips, the new, fast cycle runs.
Why does the rider brake? He hears its breath, behind,
He races on; the blurring wheels gleam.
Harshly it blows, yet it lopes after him
Past every elm and gate, mile after mile.

Then, when he rushes in, no longer hot
With clear, scared eyes, they listen; then they nod.
Almost amused, they tell him, what he saw
Was the Black Dog.
                It is seen everywhere:
But where I started, grew the calm idea
That under berried hedges, padding dark
It comes to keep you safe: to friend the night.

So much quick time lies wasted. So much fear –
Of wind, that cuts you, that could light you through,
Of quiet spiders spinning in the sun,
Of dark. There as he looked (though it was gone)
Over the plaited hawthorn reared the moon,
Lifted, through threads of cloud, a beating light.

You wriggle to the floor. Older than you
Stories do not stay still. They melt, like snow,
Trickle through books, to shine along my shelf.
In times of thaw, wandering indoors or out,
You may meet blacker dogs inside yourself.

# The New Dog

*Linda Pastan (b. 1932)*

Into the gravity of my life,
the serious ceremonies
of polish and paper
and pen, has come

this manic animal
whose innocent disruptions
make nonsense
of my old simplicities –

as if I needed him
to prove again that after
all the careful planning,
anything can happen.

# Les Petits Chiens de Paris

*Helen Burke (b. 1953)*

are everywhere.
They adorn the ladies' arms, they trot behind
the men buying baguettes.
They travel in small baskets across the Bois de Boulogne.
They look as snug as a bug in a chocolat rug.
Life is fantastique – life is unique – they bark.
Some live on the Left Bank and some live on the Right –
Les petits chiens de Paris.
They dip their feet in the fountains at the Louvre,
they lie spreadeagled against the sun dials at the Tuileries –
exquisite. Enjoying a hearty picnic.
They pose for paintings that their owners will adore
and compare to the blue dancers of Degas.
They bark at fleas at flea markets, they know why
the Mona Lisa smiles. Les petits chiens de Paris –
they travel in Vuitton handbags, in le sac next to le Blackberry,
In their one paw, fromage; in the other a glass of wine.
None of them speaks English and all of them – très beau.
They are all so chic – they nibble doggie chocolates
at midnight. The sun shines in all their eyes. Exquisite.

# The Little Dog's Day

*Rupert Brooke (1887–1915)*

All in the town were still asleep,
When the sun came up with a shout and a leap.
In the lonely streets unseen by man,
A little dog danced. And the day began.
All his life he'd been good, as far as he could,
And the poor little beast had done all that he should.
But this morning he swore, by Odin and Thor
And the Canine Valhalla – he'd stand it no more!
So his prayer he got granted – to do just what he wanted,
Prevented by none, for the space of one day.
'Jam incipiebo, sedere facebo,'
In dog-Latin he quoth, 'Euge! sophos! hurray!'
He fought with the he-dogs, and winked at the she-dogs,
A thing that had never been heard of before.
'For the stigma of gluttony, I care not a button!' he
Cried, and ate all he could swallow – and more.
He took sinewy lumps from the shins of old frumps,
And mangled the errand-boys – when he could get 'em.
He shammed furious rabies, and bit all the babies,
And followed the cats up the trees, and then ate 'em!'
They thought 'twas the devil was holding a revel,
And sent for the parson to drive him away;
For the town never knew such a hullabaloo
As that little dog raised – till the end of that day.

When the blood-red sun had gone burning down,
And the lights were lit in the little town,
Outside, in the gloom of the twilight grey,
The little dog died when he'd had his day.

# Lone Dog
*Irene Rutherford McLeod (1891–1968)*

I'm a lean dog, a keen dog, a wild dog, and lone;
I'm a rough dog, a tough dog, hunting on my own;
I'm a bad dog, a mad dog, teasing silly sheep;
I love to sit and bay the moon, to keep fat souls from sleep.

I'll never be a lap dog, licking dirty feet,
A sleek dog, a meek dog, cringing for my meat,
Not for me the fireside, the well-filled plate,
But shut door, and sharp stone, and cuff and kick, and hate.

Not for me the other dogs, running by my side,
Some have run a short while, but none of them would bide.
O mine is still the lone trail, the hard trail, the best,
Wide wind, and wild stars, and hunger of the quest!

# Dog

*Lawrence Ferlinghetti (b. 1919)*

The dog trots freely in the street
and sees reality
and the things he sees
are bigger than himself
and the things he sees
are his reality
Drunks in doorways
Moons on trees
The dog trots freely thru the streets
and the things he sees
are smaller than himself
Fish on newsprint
Ants in holes
Chickens in Chinatown windows
their heads a block away
The dog trots freely in the street
and the things he smells
smell something like himself
The dog trots freely in the streets
past puddles and babies
cats and cigars
pool rooms and policemen
He doesn't hate cops
He merely has no use for them
and he goes past them

and past the dead cows hung up whole
in front of the San Francisco Meat Market
he would rather eat a tender cow
than a tough policeman
though either might do
And he goes past the Romeo Ravioli Factory
and past Coit's Tower
but he's not afraid of Congressman Doyle
although what he hears is very discouraging
very depressing
very absurd
to a sad young dog like himself
to a serious dog like himself
But he has his own free world to live in
His own fleas to eat
He will not be muzzled
Congressman Doyle is just another
fire hydrant
to him
The dog trots freely in the street
and has his own dog's life to live
and to think about
and to reflect upon
touching and tasting and testing everything
investigating everything
without benefit of perjury
a real realist
with a real tale to tell
and a real tail to tell it with

a real live
      barking
            democratic dog
engaging in real
         free enterprise
with something to say
           about ontology
something to say
    about reality
         and how to see it
           and how to hear it
With his head cocked sideways
         at streetcorners
as if he is just about to have
      his picture taken
         for Victor Records
   listening for
      His Master's Voice
  and looking
      like a living questionmark
      into the
      great gramophone
      of puzzling existence
with its wondrous hollow horn
  which always seems
just about to spout forth
        some Victorious answer
       to everything

# Pluviophile

*Wendy Pratt (b. 1978)*

When it comes, thick and soft
as the pelt of an animal,
I am grounded, brought down
to calm in the smell of damp earth.
We wait like the wet starlings
under tree cover, their song-work
undone in the shallow hiss
of leaves and rain. I am paused,
smelling the green of the grass,
the hung heads of daffodils,
watching the plough-furrows
fill with water. A dog barks
somewhere, on one of the farms,
and the spaniel lifts his wet head, waits
as I wait – we are communed,
marooned, standing peacefully,
watching the water make mud
out of soil, movement out of stillness.

# The Dogs at Live Oak Beach, Santa Cruz

*Alicia Ostriker (b. 1937)*

As if there could be a world
Of absolute innocence
In which we forget ourselves

The owners throw sticks
And half-bald tennis balls
Toward the surf
And the happy dogs leap after them
As if catapulted –

Black dogs, tan dogs,
Tubes of glorious muscle –

Pursuing pleasure
More than obedience
They race, skid to a halt in the wet sand,
Sometimes they'll plunge straight into
The foaming breakers

Like diving birds, letting the green turbulence
Toss them, until they snap and sink

Teeth into floating wood
Then bound back to their owners
Shining wet, with passionate speed
For nothing,
For absolutely nothing but joy.

# The Dog Parade

*Arthur Guiterman (1871–1943)*

In times of calm or hurricane, in days of sun or shower,
The dog-paraders, each and all, observe the canine hour,

And, some with pups in single leash, and some with
    tugging pairs,
Take out their poodles, pointers, Poms and frisky
    wirehairs.

The Scotties patter doggedly, sedate and wistful-eyed,
The setters leap, the spaniels romp, the Great Danes
    walk in pride.

And here are shaggy shepherd dogs, those heroes
     of the farm,
And there a Russian wolfhound comes with quaint,
     Slavonic charm.

Or one may note a brindled bull, less frivolous than most,
Who, like a faithful sentinel, is ever at his post.

But still the dog-paraders march, exchanging friendly bows,
Escorting dachshunds, Dobermans, Dalmatians, Pekes
     and chows.

And still in placid dignity that nothing can disturb,
They lead their charges down the street, and sometimes
     to the curb.

# Dogs and Weather
*Winifred Welles (1893–1939)*

I'd like a different dog
  For every kind of weather –
A narrow greyhound for a fog,
  A wolfhound strange and white,
With a tail like a silver feather
  To run with in the night,
When snow is still, and winter stars are bright.

In the fall I'd like to see
  In answer to my whistle,
A golden spaniel look at me.
  But best of all for rain
A terrier, hairy as a thistle,
  To trot with fine disdain
Beside me down the soaked, sweet-smelling lane.

# The Dog

*Ogden Nash (1902–1971)*

The truth I do not stretch or shove,
When I state that the dog is full of love.
I've also found, by actual test,
A wet dog is the lovingest.

# A Popular Personage at Home

*Thomas Hardy (1840–1928)*

'I live here: "Wessex" is my name:
I am a dog known rather well:
I guard the house; but how that came
To be my whim I cannot tell.

'With a leap and a heart elate I go
At the end of an hour's expectancy
To take a walk of a mile or so
With the folk I let live here with me.

'Along the path, amid the grass
I sniff, and find out rarest smells
For rolling over as I pass
The open fields towards the dells.

'No doubt I shall always cross this sill,
And turn the corner, and stand steady,
Gazing back for my mistress till
She reaches where I have run already,

'And that this meadow with its brook,
And bulrush, even as it appears
As I plunge by with hasty look,
Will stay the same a thousand years.'

Thus 'Wessex'. But a dubious ray
At times informs his steadfast eye,
Just for a trice, as though to say,
'Yet, will this pass, and pass shall I?'

# Walking the Dog

*Howard Nemerov (1920–1991)*


Two universes mosey down the street
Connected by love and a leash and nothing else.
Mostly I look at lamplight through the leaves
While he mooches along with tail up and snout down,
Getting a secret knowledge through the nose
Almost entirely hidden from my sight.

We stand while he's enraptured by a bush
Till I can't stand our standing any more
And haul him off; for our relationship
Is patience balancing to this side tug
And that side drag; a pair of symbionts
Contented not to think each other's thoughts.

What else we have in common's what he taught,
Our interest in shit. We know its every state
From steaming fresh through stink to nature's way
Of sluicing it downstreet dissolved in rain
Or drying it to dust that blows away.
We move along the street inspecting it.

His sense of it is keener far than mine,
And only when he finds the place precise
He signifies by sniffing urgently
And circles thrice about, and squats, and shits,
Whereon we both with dignity walk home
And just to show who's master I write the poem.

# *from* A Midsummer Night's Dream

*William Shakespeare (1564–1616)*

HIPPOLYTA:

I was with Hercules and Cadmus once,
When in a wood of Crete they bay'd the bear
With hounds of Sparta: never did I hear
Such gallant chiding; for, besides the groves,
The skies, the fountains, every region near
Seem'd all one mutual cry: I never heard
So musical a discord, such sweet thunder.

THESEUS:

My hounds are bred out of the Spartan kind,
So flew'd, so sanded; and their heads are hung
With ears that sweep away the morning dew;
Crook-knee'd, and dew-lapp'd like Thessalian bulls;
Slow in pursuit, but match'd in mouth like bells,
Each under each. A cry more tuneable
Was never holla'd to, nor cheer'd with horn,
In Crete, in Sparta, nor in Thessaly:
Judge when you hear.

# To a Black Greyhound

*Julian Grenfell (1888–1915)*

Shining black in the shining light,
   Inky black in the golden sun,
Graceful as the swallow's flight,
   Light as swallow, wingèd one,
Swift as driven hurricane –
   Double-sinewed stretch and spring,
Muffled thud of flying feet,
   See the black dog galloping,
   Hear his wild foot-beat.

See him lie when the day is dead,
   Black curves curled on the boarded floor.
Sleepy eyes, my sleepy-head –
   Eyes that were aflame before.
Gentle now, they burn no more;
   Gentle now and softly warm,
With the fire that made them bright
   Hidden – as when after storm
   Softly falls the night.

God of speed, who makes the fire –
  God of Peace, who lulls the same –
God who gives the fierce desire,
  Lust for blood as fierce as flame –
God who stands in Pity's name –
  Many may ye be or less,
Ye who rule the earth and sun:
  Gods of strength and gentleness,
  Ye are ever one.

# The Lurcher

*William Cowper (1731–1800)*

Forth goes the woodman, leaving unconcerned
The cheerful haunts of men to wield the axe
And drive the wedge in yonder forest drear,
From morn to eve his solitary task.
Shaggy and lean and shrewd, with pointed ears
And tail cropped short, half-lurcher and half-cur,
His dog attends him. Close behind his heel
Now creeps he slow, and now with many a frisk
Wide scampering, snatches up the drifted snow
With ivory teeth, or ploughs it with his snout;
Then shakes his powder'd coat, and barks for joy.

# Paws on the Snow

*Roger Stevens (b. 1948)*

We are huskies
we are ready and waiting
for there's no better feeling
in the midnight sun
than the jingling and the jangling
and the scent of the tundra
and the yelps and the growling
of everyone

There's ice in the air
and the sled is ready
and the humans are on board
and Togo's the one
who will lead us as we rush
like a wind through the tundra
through the crisp and the crunch
of the snow-blinding sun
and *Mush!* Off we go
and there's no better feeling
and the wilderness is calling
and the snow starts falling
and we are born to run

# Tom's Little Dog

*Walter de la Mare (1873–1956)*

Tom told his dog called Tim to beg,
And up at once he sat,
His two clear amber eyes fixed fast,
His haunches on his mat.
Tom poised a lump of sugar on
His nose; then, 'Trust!' says he;
Stiff as a guardsman sat his Tim;
Never a hair stirred he.

'Paid for!' says Tom; and in a trice
Up jerked that moist black nose;
A snap of teeth, a crunch, a munch,
And down the sugar goes!

# The Hairy Dog

*Herbert Asquith (1881–1947)*

My dog's so furry I've not seen
His face for years and years;
His eyes are buried out of sight,
I only guess his ears.

When people ask me for his breed,
I do not know or care;
He has the beauty of them all
Hidden beneath his hair.

# Maggie

*Anon*

There was a small maiden named Maggie,
Whose dog was enormous and shaggy;
The front end of him
Looked vicious and grim –
But the tail end was friendly and waggy.

# Barry, the St Bernard

*Samuel Rogers (1763–1855)*

When the storm

Rose, and the snow rolled on in ocean-waves,
When on his face the experienced traveller fell,
Sheltering his lips and nostrils with his hands,
Then all was changed; and, sallying with their pack
Into that blank of nature, they became
Unearthly beings. 'Anselm, higher up,
Just where it drifts, a dog howls loud and long,
And now, as guided by a voice from Heaven,
Digs with his feet. That noble vehemence,
Whose can it be, but his who never erred?
A man lies underneath! Let us to work.'

# Full of the Moon

*Karla Kuskin (1932–2009)*

It's full of the moon
The dogs dance out
Through brush and bush and bramble.
They howl and yowl
And growl and prowl.
They amble, ramble, scramble.
They rush through brush.
They push through bush.
They yip and yap and hurr.
They lark around and bark around
With prickles in their fur.
They two-step in the meadow.
They polka on the lawn.
Tonight's the night
The dogs dance out
And chase their tails till dawn.

# The Kindness of Dogs

*Helen Burke (b. 1953)*

You say it and it is true.
Dogs are kind.
They buy small dog treats for each other.
They hold doors open for cats.
They run rings around the moon,
bury the sun in the sand and throw sticks
for the stars.
Dogs are kind.
They put paws on your knees on bad days.
They hold a light out to you in their eyes.
They run to the top of the mountain and bark
'Which stone did you want? Which one?'
and race back down with it and place it gently at your feet.
Dogs are kind (you say it and it is true).
They bark in all the right places at the theatre and hide
behind the sofa in the scary movie. They share their ice cream
with you, no questions asked.
Our dog – Zorro – the one we have not met yet
will be our best chum, best in the whole world.
He will be faithful and strong.
In dreams he runs right up to me, barks and says:

'You look a little peaky, why not take a year off
and come with me to Zanzibar. Stretch your legs
    and chase
your tail. See all that world out there? It's yours for
    the asking.'
And he gives me one of his fleas as a token of goodwill.
Dogs are kind.
They run into the sea and look amazed that it is wet
but they do not take offence.
They love a through-breeze in their ears, hanging out
    of windows,
a breeze that says they're happy in all the different
    continents.
Dogs are good map-readers and they always
know a better route – past the poodle beauty parlour
    and turn
right at the Dog and Duck.
Dogs lay their heads beside you and know just what
    you're thinking.
Dogs' favourite word is walk.
Dogs are kind.

# Not My Dog

*Matt Harvey*


*You're not my dog*
But I could be. I would be, if you'd have me.

I'd be your very good boy

I would, I would. I would!
*You're not my dog*
We could do such things together

We could we could we could though.

Couldn't we?

*I'm not even a dog person.*
Amazing. That's my favourite. Nor am I!

I'm a people puppy. A really good boy!

Am I good boy? I am! I am! I am!

And I'm yours.

*You're not my dog!*
O love the way you say that, it's so funny!

It's the best fun ever being your dog.

*YOU'RE NOT MY DOG*
Love it!

You're the best owner I've ever had.

Ever.

# The Best Moment of the Night

*Tony Hoagland (b. 1953)*

You had a moment with the dog,
down near the base of the butcher-block table
just as the party was getting started.

Just as the guests were bringing in
their potluck salads and vegetarian lasagna,
setting them down on the buffet,

you had an unforeseeable exchange of warmth
with this scruffy, bug-eyed creature
who let you scratch his ears.

He lives down there, among the high heels
and the cowboy boots, below the human roar
rising to its boil up above. Like his, your evening

is just beginning – but you
are lonelier than him. You think
that if you disappeared tonight,

you would not be missed for years;
yet here, the licking of the hands and face;
and here, the baring of the vulnerable belly.

You are still panting, and alive, and seeking love;
yet no one who knows you
knows, somehow,

about your wet, black nose,
or that you can wag your tail.

# Verse for a Certain Dog

*Dorothy Parker (1893–1967)*

Such glorious faith as fills your limpid eyes,
    Dear little friend of mine, I never knew.
All-innocent are you, and yet all-wise.
    (For Heaven's sake, stop worrying that shoe!)
You look about, and all you see is fair;
    This mighty globe was made for you alone.
Of all the thunderous ages, you're the heir.
    (Get off the pillow with that dirty bone!)

A skeptic world you face with steady gaze;
    High in young pride you hold your noble head;
Gayly you meet the rush of roaring days.
    (*Must* you eat puppy biscuit on the bed?)
Lancelike your courage, gleaming swift and strong,
    Yours the white rapture of a wingèd soul,
Yours is a spirit like a May-day song.
    (God help you, if you break the goldfish bowl!)

'Whatever is, is good' – your gracious creed.
    You wear your joy of living like a crown.
Love lights your simplest act, your every deed.
    (Drop it, I tell you – put that kitten down!)
You are God's kindliest gift of all – a friend.
    Your shining loyalty unflecked by doubt,
You ask but leave to follow to the end.
    (Couldn't you wait until I took you out?)

# Lost Dog

*Ellen Bass (b. 1947)*

It's just getting dark, fog drifting in,
damp grasses fragrant with anise and mint,
and though I call his name
until my voice cracks,
there's no faint tinkling
of tag against collar, no sleek
black silhouette with tall ears rushing
toward me through the wild radish.

As it turns out, he's trotted home,
tracing the route of his trusty urine.
Now he sprawls on the deep red rug, not dead,
not stolen by a car on West Cliff Drive.

Every time I look at him, the wide head
resting on outstretched paws,
joy does another lap around the racetrack
of my heart. Even in sleep
when I turn over to ease my bad hip,
I'm suffused with contentment.

If I could lose him like this every day
I'd be the happiest woman alive.

# I Am His Highness' Dog at Kew

*Alexander Pope (1688–1744)*

'I am his Highness' dog at Kew,
Pray tell me sir, whose dog are you?'

# Dog
*Helen (14)*


Dog,
you are sleeping
and the sky is turning like a music box
my heart is beating like ship's timber
and I am struggling with basic French.
Your legs paddle through a squirrel chase
a race through water, underground, through
the holes in the clock faces to
another day where I sit here again, telling you things –
like how when I stand on the lawn in the dark
with the kitchen light on, in my muddy shoes
I am standing in another time.
You stop your chase, I stop my nonsense.
*How was your day*, I ask. You roll over.
*Me too.*

# The Dog

*Aracelis Girmay (b. 1977)*


Yes. I will watch your dog
while you are away in Antarctica & Belarus.
It will be my pleasure to take him out
into the morning & into the night grown
thick as wild crop after rain. Probably,
he will love it, but will miss you with his face
at the window near the door he last saw you leave from.
He will sleep there, waiting, night after night,
as my own Lola does when I am gone, & in his head,
he will make a list of things he knows you'll come back for.
He will say, Come back, come back
for the shoe you left, & the telephone.
Come back, he will say, to ride in a car
& to throw a ball. Come back for the radio.
& one of these nights he will notice the moon
& it will be full, & he will call it Antarctica
& will feel better knowing you are there
some where he can see.
This will be his way of coping.
& when you come back, you know the story:
your work-boots, glistened by a travel,
will stand coolly underneath you
at the front door, & the dogs,
your dog & my dog, will howl

to meet you. & won't you come
with your deep pockets filled with souvenirs of ice
that, later, in the kitchen, you will call 'fruit'
as you slice into its brilliant, shining meat
with a hot silver knife. & the dog
will lick the ice with his tongue, & turn
his good head toward the window
& he will think Antarctica is lonely, & the light
will push through him
with a sadness that herds sadness
into the bell of his dog heart,
a heart you'll want to throw your arms around
for the way it knows what it is to be so swollen with loss,
for the way it knows that every night, heaven will sing,
& every morning, heaven will sing like this,
at the windows. & the dog
will put his giant, breathing face into your palm
& for one moment, no sad thing will creep
or move ominously into the continent of the dog
whose mastiff lungs are filled with you now. Call it
the memory's inventory: his lungs will hold,
like saddlebags, your hundred smells of flowers & work
& chutneys & schoolyards & gasoline.
He will forget that to see you leave
burned down his ramshackle heart once, instead
your smells will flood him in tides craned down
toward the chest's burning honeycomb, amen,
perfect as water rushing toward thirst, again, amen.

# Mongrel Heart

*David Baker (b. 1954)*

Up the dog bounds to the window, baying
   like a basset his doleful, tearing sounds
      from the belly, as if mourning a dead king,

and now he's howling like a beagle – yips, brays,
   gagging growls – and scratching the sill paintless,
      that's how much he's missed you, the two of you,

both of you, mother and daughter, my wife
   and child. All week he's curled at my feet,
      warming himself and me watching more TV,

or wandered the lonely rooms, my dog shadow,
   who like a poodle now hops, amped-up windup
      maniac yo-yo with matted curls and snot nose

smearing the panes, having heard another car
   like yours taking its grinding turn down
      our block, or a school bus, or bird-squawk,

that's how much he's missed you, good dog,
   companion dog, dog-of-all-types, most excellent dog
      I told you once and for all we should never get.

# The Dog

*Edgar A. Guest (1881–1959)*

I like a dog at my feet when I read,
whatever his size or whatever his breed.
A dog now and then that will nuzzle my hand
As though I were the greatest of men in the land,
And trying to tell me it's pleasant to be
On such intimate terms with a fellow like me.

I like a dog at my side when I eat,
I like to give him a bit of my meat;
And though mother objects and insists it is bad
To let dogs in the dining room, still I am glad
To behold him stretched out on the floor by my chair.
It's cheering to see such a faithful friend there.

A dog leads a curious life at the best.
By the way of his tail is his pleasure expressed.
He pays a high tribute to man when he stays
True to his friend to the end of his days.
And I wonder sometimes if it happens to be
That dogs pay no heed of the faults which men see.

Should I prove a failure, should I stoop to wrong;
Be weak at a time when I should have been strong,
Should I lose my money, the gossips would sneer
And fill with my blundering many an ear,
But still, as I opened my door, I should see
My dog wag his tail with a welcome for me.

# Fidelity of the Dog

*William Wordsworth (1770–1850)*

A barking sound the shepherd hears,
   A cry as of a dog or fox;
He halts, and searches with his eyes
   Among the scattered rocks:
And now at distance can discern
A stirring in a brake of fern;
And instantly a dog is seen,
Glancing through that covert green.

The dog is not of mountain breed;
   Its motions too are wild and shy;
With something, as the shepherd thinks,
   Unusual in its cry.
Nor is there anyone in sight
All round, in hollow, or on height;
Nor shout, nor whistle, strikes his ear;
What is the creature doing here?

It was a cove, a huge recess,
   That keeps till June December's snow;
A lofty precipice in front,
   A silent tarn below!
Far in the bosom of Helvellyn,
Remote from public road or dwelling,
Pathway, or cultivated land,
From trace of human foot or hand.

There sometimes doth a leaping fish
    Send through the tarn a lonely cheer;
The crags repeat the raven's croak,
    In symphony austere;
Thither the rainbow comes – the cloud –
And mists that spread the flying shroud;
And sunbeams; and the sounding blast,
That, if it could, would hurry past,
But that enormous barrier binds it fast.

Not free from boding thoughts, a while
    The Shepherd stood: then makes his way
Toward the Dog, o'er rocks and stones,
    As quickly as he may;
Nor far had gone, before he found
A human skeleton on the ground;
The appalled discoverer with a sigh
Looks round, to learn the history.

From those abrupt and perilous rocks
    The Man had fallen, that place of fear!
At length upon the Shepherd's mind
    It breaks, and all is clear:
He instantly recalled the name,
And who he was, and whence he came;
Remembered, too, the very day
On which the traveller passed this way.

But hear a wonder, for whose sake
    This lamentable tale I tell!
A lasting monument of words
    This wonder merits well.
The Dog, which still was hovering nigh,
Repeating the same timid cry,
This Dog had been through three months space
A dweller in that savage place.

Yes, proof was plain that, since the day
    When this ill-fated traveller died,
The Dog had watched about the spot,
    Or by his master's side:
How nourished here through such long time
He knows, who gave that love sublime;
And gave that strength of feeling, great
Above all human estimate.

# The Home-Loving Dog

*Matthew Prior (1664–1721)*

The lonely fox roams far abroad,
On secret rapine bent, and midnight fraud;
Now haunts the cliff, now traverses the lawn,
And flies the hated neighbourhood of man:
While the kind spaniel, or the faithful hound,
Likest that fox in shape and species found,
Refuses through these cliffs and lawns to roam,
Pursues the noted path, and covets home;
Does with kind joy domestic faces meet,
Take what the glutted child denies to eat,
And, dying, licks his long-loved master's feet.

# A Friendly Welcome

*George Gordon, Lord Byron (1788–1824)*

'Tis sweet to hear the watch-dog's honest bark
Bay deep-mouthed welcome as we draw near home;
'Tis sweet to know there is an eye will mark
Our coming, and look brighter when we come.

# Argus

*Alexander Pope (1688–1744)*

When wise Ulysses, from his native coast
Long kept by wars, and long by tempests tost,
Arrived at last – poor, old, disguised, alone,
To all his friends and ev'n his queen unknown,
Changed as he was, with age, and toils, and cares,
Furrowed his rev'rend face, and white his hairs,
In his own palace forced to ask his bread,
Scorned by those slaves his former bounty fed,
Forgot of all his own domestic crew,
His faithful dog his rightful master knew!
Unfed, unhoused, neglected, on the clay,
Like an old servant, now cashiered, he lay;
And though ev'n then expiring on the plain,
Touched with resentment of ungrateful man,
And longing to behold his ancient lord again.
Him when he saw, he rose, and crawled to meet,
('Twas all he could), and fawned, and kissed his feet,
Seized with dumb joy; then falling by his side,
Owned his returning lord, looked up, and died.

# Fellowship in Grief

*Thomas Aird (1802–1876)*

Loved and loving, God her trust,
The shepherd's wife goes dust to dust;
Their dog, his eye half sad, half prompt to save.
Follows the coffin down into the grave.
Behind his man he takes his drooping stand,
The clods jar hollow on the coffin lid:
    Startled, he lifts his head;
To that quick shudder of his master's pain,
He thrusts his muzzle deep into his hand
    Solicitous, deeper, yet again.

No kind old pressure answers; shrinking back
Apart, perplexed with broken ties,
Yet loyal, grave-ward down he lies,
His muzzle flat along the snowy track.
The mourners part. The widowed shepherd goes
Homeward, yet homeless, through the mountain snows.
    Him follows slowly, silently,
That dog. What a strange trouble in his eyes –
    Something beyond relief!
Is it the creature yearning in dumb stress
To burst obstruction up to consciousness,
    And fellowship in reason's grief?

# O Pug!

*Stevie Smith (1902–1971)*

*To the Brownes' pug dog, on my lap, in their car,*
*coming home from Norfolk.*

O Pug, some people do not like you,
But I like you,
Some people say you do not breathe, you snore,
I don't mind,
One person says he is always conscious of your behind,
Is that your fault?

Your own people love you,
All the people in the family that owns you
Love you: Good pug, they cry, Happy pug,
Pug-come-for-a-walk.

You are an old dog now
And in all your life
You have never had cause for a moment's anxiety,
Yet,
In those great eyes of yours,
Those liquid and protuberant orbs,
Lies the shadow of immense insecurity. There
Panic walks.

Yes, yes, I know,
When your mistress is with you,
When your master
Takes you upon his lap,
Just then, for a moment,
Almost you are not frightened.

But at heart you are frightened, you always have been.

O Pug, obstinate old nervous breakdown,
In the midst of so much love,
And such comfort,
Still to feel unsafe and be afraid,

How one's heart goes out to you!

# The Frolicsome Old Dog

*John Clare (1793–1864)*

The barking dogs, by lane and wood,
Drive sheep afield from foddering ground;
And Echo, in her summer mood,
Briskly mocks the cheering sound.

No more behind his master's heels
The dog creeps on his winter-pace;
But cocks his tail, and o'er the fields
Runs many a wild and random chase,

Following, in spite of chiding calls,
The startled cat with harmless glee,
Scaring her up the weed-green walls,
Or mossy-mottled apple tree.

As crows from morning perches fly,
He barks and follows them in vain;
Even larks will catch his nimble eye,
And off he starts and barks again,
With breathless haste and blinded guess,
Oft following where the hare hath gone;
Forgetting, in his joy's excess,
His frolic puppy-days are done!

# The Best Friend

*Meribah Abbott (1863–1923)*

If I was sad, then he had grief, as well –
Seeking my hands with soft insistent paw,
Searching my face with anxious eyes that saw
More than my halting, human speech could tell;
Eyes wide with wisdom, fine, compassionate –
Dear, loyal one, that knew not wrong nor hate.

If I made merry – then how he would strive
To show his joy; 'Good master, let's to play,
The world is ours,' that gladsome bark would say;
'Just yours and mine – 'tis fun to be alive!'
Our world ... four walls above the city's din,
My crutch the bar that ever held us in.

Whate'er my mood – the fretful word, or sweet,
The swift command, the wheedling undertone,
His faith was fixed, his love was mine, alone,
His heaven was here at my slow crippled feet:
Oh, friend thrice-lost; oh, fond heart unassailed,
Ye taught me trust when man's dull logic failed.

# Our Dog Jock

*James Payn (1830–1898)*

A rollicksome frolicsome rare old cock
As ever did nothing was our dog Jock;
A gleesome, fleasome, affectionate beast,
As slow at a fight, as swift at a feast;
A wit among dogs, when his life 'gan fail,
One couldn't but see the old wag in his tale,
When his years grew long and his eyes grew dim,
And his course of bark could not strengthen him.
Never more now shall our knees be pressed
By his dear old chops in their slobbery rest,
Nor our mirth be stirred at his solemn looks,
As wise, and as dull, as divinity books.
Our old friend's dead, but we all well know
He's gone to the Kennels where the good dogs go,
Where the cooks be not, but the beef-bones be,
And his old head never need turn for a flea.

# Exemplary Nick

*Sydney Smith (1771–1845)*

Here lies poor Nick, an honest creature,
Of faithful, gentle, courteous nature;
A parlour pet unspoiled by favour,
A pattern of good dog behaviour.
Without a wish, without a dream,
Beyond his home and friends at Cheam,
Contentedly through life he trotted
Along the path that fate allotted;
Till Time, his aged body wearing,
Bereaved him of his sight and hearing,
Then laid him down without a pain
To sleep, and never wake again.

# The Power of the Dog

*Rudyard Kipling (1865–1936)*

There is sorrow enough in the natural way
From men and women to fill our day;
And when we are certain of sorrow in store,
Why do we always arrange for more?
Brothers and Sisters, I bid you beware
Of giving your heart to a dog to tear.

Buy a pup and your money will buy
Love unflinching that cannot lie –
Perfect passion and worship fed
By a kick in the ribs or a pat on the head.
Nevertheless it is hardly fair
To risk your heart for a dog to tear.

When the fourteen years which Nature permits
Are closing in asthma, or tumour, or fits,
And the vet's unspoken prescription runs
To lethal chambers or loaded guns,
Then you will find – it's your own affair –
But ... you've given your heart for a dog to tear.

When the body that lived at your single will,
With its whimper of welcome, is stilled (how still!);
When the spirit that answered your every mood
Is gone – wherever it goes – for good,
You will discover how much you care,
And will give your heart for the dog to tear.

We've sorrow enough in the natural way,
When it comes to burying Christian clay.
Our loves are not given, but only lent,
At compound interest of cent per cent.
Though it is not always the case, I believe,
That the longer we've kept 'em, the more do we grieve:
For, when debts are payable, right or wrong,
A short-time loan is as bad as a long –
So why in Heaven (before we are there)
Should we give our hearts to a dog to tear?

# Credits

Rehomer's Prayer © Di Slaney/Valley Press

Dog, on First Being Named © Jane Commane/ Bloodaxe Books

Macbeth (Act 3, Scene 1) – William Shakespeare (public domain)

A Little Dog Sense © Sue Hardy-Dawson

The Song of the Dog Quoodle – G. K. Chesterton (public domain)

Flush or Faunus – Elizabeth Barrett Browning (public domain)

Bibbles – D. H. Lawrence (public domain)

We Meet at Morn, My Dog and I – Hardwicke Drummond Rawnsley (public domain)

Flight © Lisa Oliver

I Started Early, Took My Dog – Emily Dickinson (public domain)

Roads – Amy Lowell (public domain)

The Invitation: To Tom Hughes – Charles Kingsley (public domain)

Dog – Harold Monro (public domain)

The Little White Dog – May Ellis Nichols (public domain)

Golden Retrievals – Mark Doty (Reproduced by permission of HarperCollins Publishers)

They (may forget (their names (if let out))) © Vahni Capildeo/Carcanet Press

Uncertainty is Not a Good Dog – Jo Shapcott (Reproduced by permission of Faber & Faber, Ltd.)

Black Dog © Alison Brackenbury/Carcanet Press

The New Dog © Linda Pastan/W. W. Norton & Company, Inc.

Les Petits Chiens de Paris © Helen Burke/Valley Press

The Little Dog's Day – Rupert Brooke (public domain)

Lone Dog – Irene Rutherford McLeod © Estate of I. R. de Selincourt

Dog – Lawrence Ferlinghetti (Reproduced by permission of New Directions Publishing Corp.)

Pluviophile © Wendy Pratt/Valley Press

The Dogs at Live Oak Beach, Santa Cruz © Alicia Ostriker/ University of Pittsburgh Press

The Dog Parade – Arthur Guiterman (public domain)

Dogs and Weather – Winifred Welles (public domain)

The Dog – Ogden Nash © Estate of Ogden Nash

A Popular Personage at Home – Thomas Hardy (public domain)

Walking the Dog – Howard Nemerov (Reproduced by permission of Margaret Nemerov)

A Midsummer Night's Dream – William Shakespeare (public domain)

To a Black Greyhound – Julian Grenfell (public domain)

The Lurcher – William Cowper (public domain)

Paws on the Snow © Roger Stevens/Otter-Barry Books

Tom's Little Dog – Walter de la Mare (Reproduced by permission of the Literary Trustees of Walter de la Mare and the Society of Authors)

The Hairy Dog – Herbert Asquith (public domain)

Maggie – Anon (public domain)

Barry, the St Bernard – Samuel Rogers (public domain)

Full of the Moon © Karla Kuskin/ScottTreimel NY

The Kindness of Dogs © Helen Burke/Valley Press

Not My Dog © Matt Harvey

The Best Moment of the Night – Tony Hoagland (Reproduced by permission of Kathleen Lee)

Verse for a Certain Dog – Dorothy Parker (Reproduced by permission of Penguin Random House LLC)

Lost Dog © Ellen Bass/Copper Canyon Press

His Highness' Dog at Kew – Alexander Pope (public domain)

Dog – Helen (14) (Reproduced by permission of Kate Clanchy)

The Dog © Aracelis Girmay/Northwestern University Press

Mongrel Heart © David Baker

The Dog © Edgar A. Guest/Penguin Random House LLC

Fidelity of the Dog – William Wordsworth (public domain)

The Home-Loving Dog – Matthew Prior (public domain)

A Friendly Welcome – George Gordon, Lord Byron (public domain)

Argus – Alexander Pope (public domain)

Fellowship in Grief – Thomas Aird (public domain)

O Pug! – Stevie Smith (Reproduced by permission of Faber & Faber, Ltd.)

The Frolicsome Old Dog – John Clare (public domain)

The Best Friend – Meribah Abbott (public domain)

Our Dog Jock – James Payn (public domain)

Exemplary Nick – Sydney Smith (public domain)

The Power of the Dog – Rudyard Kipling (public domain)

# Bibliography

*A Dog Runs Through It* by Linda Pastan (W. W. Norton & Company, 2018)

*Assembly Lines* by Jane Commane (Bloodaxe, 2018)

*Doggerel: Poems about Dogs* (Everyman's Library, 2003)

*Dog Poems by The World's Greatest Poets* (Serpent's Tail, 2019)

*Emily Dickinson's Poems: As She Preserved Them* by Emily Dickinson (Harvard University Press, 2016)

*Fire to Fire: New and Selected Poems* by Mark Doty (Harper Perennial, 2009)

*Gifts the Mole Gave Me* by Wendy Pratt (Valley Press, 2017)

*In the Middle of Trees* by Karla Kuskin (Harper, 1958)

*I Wandered Lonely as a Cloud... and Other Poems You Half-Remember from* School edited by Ana Sampson (Michael O'Mara Books, 2009)

*Poems for Happiness* (Macmillan Collector's Library, 2019)

*Poems of Childhood* (Macmillan Collector's Library, 2019)

*Poems of Thomas Hardy* by Thomas Hardy (Macmillan, 1979)

*Reward for Winter* by Di Slaney (Valley Press, 2016)

*Sit!* by Matt Harvey and Claudia Schmid (Unicorn, 2019)

*Sixty Women Poets* edited by Linda France (Bloodaxe, 1993)

*Teeth* by Aracelis Girmay (Northwestern University Press, 2007)

*The Dog in British Poetry* edited by R. Maynard Leonard (Chronicle Books, 2005)

*The Everyday Poet: Poems to Live By* edited by Deborah Alma (Michael O'Mara Books, 2016)

*The Human Line* by Ellen Bass (Copper Canyon Press, 2007)

*The Waggiest Tails* by Brian Moses and Roger Stevens (Otter-Barry Books, 2018)

*Thomas Hardy: The Complete Poems* (Macmillan, 1979)

*Today the Birds Will Sing: Collected Poems 1969-2016* by Helen Burke (Valley Press, 2017)

*Venus as a Bear* by Vahni Capildeo (Carcanet Press, 2018)